INTRODUCTION

Oh, what to cook? We are spoiled for choice when it comes to cooking, we have a multitude of fresh fruit and vegetables, herbs and spices and fresh meats of all types available to us.

This book presents you with a range of tips to get the best out of whatever type and cut of meat you choose to cook. Savor the tastes of meat cooked to perfection for your friends and family. All the recipes in this little compendium of cooking are beautifully photographed so you will know just how they will appear on your plate.

Whether you are a novice or an experienced cook, you will find all these recipes to be the perfect blend of simplicity of preparation and sophistication of flavor, and you will enjoy not only eating them but preparing them as well. Go to it, you will be so glad you did.

BEEF

PAN-FRYING BEEF

Suitable cuts: fillet, minute steak, oyster blade, rib, rib eye (scotch fillet), rump, sirloin, T-bone.

POINTS FOR SUCCESS

Trim steaks and chops of excess fat. Make one or two small cuts around selvedge, past the gristle line into the meat. This prevents meat curling up.

☛ Season with pepper and dried herbs before cooking, add salt after cooking.

☛ Use a small amount of oil in the pan, too much oil makes meat stew.

☛ A non-stick pan helps reduce the quantity of cooking fat needed, therefore reducing the fat content of the meal. Alternatively, use non-stick cooking paper to reduce the fat content and prevent the beef sticking.

☛ Oils or fats suitable for pan-frying are: vegetable oils, butter, ghee (clarified butter) and margarine. Butter gives a good flavor but can burn easily, it is better to use a combination of butter and oil to prevent this and still retain flavor. Ghee will not burn easily and has a distinctive and pleasant flavor.

☛ Heat oil and pan well. Sear meat on both sides to seal

in juices, then turn down to medium-high or medium to continue cooking. Cooking time will depend on the thickness of the meat. If the cut is thick, lower the heat to allow the center to cook. If the cut is thin, cook quickly for a short time. Stay close to the pan and adjust heat when necessary.

🍃 Cooking times vary with the thickness of the meat and the type of pan used, but a good guide is: rare: 2–3 minutes on each side, medium: 4–6 minutes on each side, well done: 6–9 minutes on each side. Turn meat three times at the most, once only for rare.

🍃 To test if cooked, do not cut with a knife as juices escape. Test meat by pressing with blunt tongs, the meat will be: rare: springy to touch, medium: firmer to touch, well done: very firm to touch.

🍃 Don't turn meat too often or use too low a heat as it will stew and toughen due to lack of time and heat needed to seal in the juices. You will know if this happens, as the meat will shed its juices.

🍃 Don't pan-fry with a lid on. The lid traps in steam, making the meat stew.

🍃 For extra tenderness and flavor, marinate meat in a wine or citrus-based marinade. For best results, place meat and marinade in a non-metallic dish, cover with lid and refrigerate for 2 hours or more, overnight if possible.

👁 Always deglaze the pan (dissolve the meat juices that have stuck to the base of the pan) with stock, water, wine, lemon or fruit juices. This makes a quick and easy sauce. Cream, sour cream or yogurt can then be added to make a richer sauce.

👁 Always remember to have vegetable and rice or pasta accompaniments cooked and ready before commencing to pan-fry the meat. On completion of cooking, panfried meat should be served immediately.

STIR-FRYING BEEF

Suitable cuts: boneless blade, fillet, round, topside, rump, rib eye (scotch fillet), sirloin.

POINTS FOR SUCCESS

👁 If preparing your own, partly freeze the meat first, this makes it easier to cut. Trim fat from the meat then slice thinly across the grain, this ensures tenderness. Cut strips 5–8cm (2–3in) in length.

👁 Marinate the strips for at least 30 minutes in a mixture of cornflour (cornstarch) blended with water, soy sauce, rice wine, or dry sherry. This helps keep in juices and adds flavor.

👁 Stir-fry meat in small batches (200–300 g/7–10½ oz) to prevent meat shedding its juices.

👁 Have all meat and vegetables prepared and all flavorings and sauces measured before starting.

☞ When ready to stir-fry, add a small quantity of oil to wok or frying pan and swirl to coat base and sides.

☞ Heat until smoking. If a wok is not available, a heavy-based frying pan may be used. Place over the small gas ring or element so that the heat is concentrated in the center of the pan.

OVEN-ROASTING BEEF

Suitable cuts: long fillet of beef, rib eye roast (scotch fillet), rump roast, bolar blade, rolled rib (rolled roast), fresh silverside, set of ribs (standing rib roast), sirloin, skirt steak (rolled). Topside may be roasted successfully if you keep it rare.

POINTS FOR SUCCESS

☞ Trim some fat from the meat. Some fat cover is necessary to keep the meat moist during cooking.

☞ Remove silver skin from beef fillet to prevent curling while cooking. Tie to keep shape.

☞ Place meat on a rack in a roasting pan. Add a cup of water or wine to cover base of pan. This will prevent the meat juices from charring. Juices may then be used in making gravy. When liquid dries out, add a little more.

☞ Roasts may be placed in a roasting pan without a rack. However, ensure there is a little water in the dish. As the roast cooks, fat will melt into the dish. Insert a meat thermometer into the thickest part of the meat. This will register the internal temperature of the meat, which will indicate how cooked it is. Calculate cooking time by the weight of the meat .

☛ Cook small or narrow roasts at 200°C (400°F), larger roasts at 180°C (350°F).

☛ Oven bags keep food moist and succulent, eliminate the need to clean the oven, and reduce the amount of washing up. When using an oven bag, the cooking times per 500g (17½oz) are: rare: 20 minutes, medium: 25 minutes, well done: 30 minutes.

☛ Very large cuts will need turning halfway through cooking.

☛ Remove cooked meat from oven, cover with foil and allow to stand 15 minutes.

This allows juices to settle and makes carving easier.

☛ Carve meat across the grain to ensure tenderness.

☛ To make gravy, skim fat from pan. Scrape all cooked-on juices from sides and base of pan, washing down with stock or water (the term for this is deglazing).

OVEN-ROASTING BEEF...

Degree of Cooking	Time per 500g / 17½oz	Internal Temperature
Rare	20-25 Minutes	60°C / 140°F
Medium	25-30 Minutes	70°C / 160°F
Well Done	30-35 Minutes	75°C / 170°F

FILLETS REQUIRE LESS TIME...

Degree of Cooking	Time per 500g / 17½oz	Internal Temperature
Rare	15-20 Minutes	60°C / 140°F
Medium	20-25 Minutes	70°C / 160°F
Well Done	25-30 Minutes	75°C / 170°F

BARBECUING BEEF

Suitable cuts: fillet, minute, oyster blade, rib, rib eye (scotch fillet), rump, sirloin, T-bone, blade, topside

Degree of Cooking	Time per 500g / 17½oz
Rare	2-3 Minutes
Medium	4-6 Minutes
Well Done	6-8 Minutes

POINTS FOR SUCCESS

- Lightly oil grill or plate to prevent meat sticking.

- Marinate steaks, if desired, to add flavor.

- To ensure tenderness for blade and topside steak, marinate in an acid-based marinade containing wine or citrus juices for 2 hours or more.

- Purchase kebabs from your local butcher already cut, or cut larger pieces into 3cm (1.2in) cubes.

- When cooking, begin on high heat to seal in juices, then reduce heat, move meat to cooler part of plate or raise the grill higher off the coals.

- Cooking times are the same as for grilling.

GRILLING BEEF

Suitable cuts: fillet, minute, oyster blade, rib, rib eye (scotch fillet), rump, T-bone, boneless sirloin.

POINTS FOR SUCCESS

- Choose steak that is a deep red color, as this indicates meat has been well aged and is tender.

- Trim meat of any fat. Slash the fat line at intervals to prevent the meat curling while cooking.

- Season steaks with pepper and herbs before cooking, sprinkle with salt after cooking. For extra flavor, the steak may be rubbed with a little crushed garlic.

👅 To keep steak moist, brush with a little olive oil just before grilling.

👅 Heat grill to very hot for approximately 5 minutes before placing the meat under. Do not leave the grill pan under the heat while heating the grill. The pan should be cold when the meat is placed on it so it will not stick.

👅 Cooking time varies according to thickness and desired degree of cooking.

👅 Do not turn meat too often, it will not have time to seal in juices and will stew.

👅 Leave grill door open while grilling.

👅 Grilled meat is quick to cook and must be served immediately. Have all accompaniments prepared before meat is placed under the grill.

MINCE BEEF

Mince meat has many cut surfaces and is therefore more vulnerable to spoilage than other meat. Extra care must be taken during transport and storage.

Transport home quickly, make it the last item on your shopping list, or take an insulated bag to place it in.

To freeze mince, place 500g (17½ oz) in a ziplock bag, expel air and seal. Label and date and use within 2 months. Flat-pack mince defrosts more quickly than a thick ball of mince. If all the pack is not to be used, a thin pack can be easily cut in half.

Do not refreeze mince that has been thawed.

POINTS FOR SUCCESS

☛ If the recipe requires mince to be browned, heat a little oil in a saucepan, add mince and stir continuously until mince changes from red to a light brown color. Mince must all break up and not form into lumps; break up lumps as they form.

☛ When using very low-fat mince, just place the mince in a saucepan and add water to make it very moist. Place on the heat and stir until mince changes from pink to grey. Add flavorings and simmer.

☛ To cook properly, mince needs to simmer for 25–30 minutes.

BRAISING, CASSEROLING AND STEWING BEEF

Suitable cuts: blade brisket, chuck, round, shin (gravy beef), fresh silverside, skirt, spare ribs.

POINTS FOR SUCCESS

☛ Buy meat in one piece so it is possible to cut into 3cm (1.2in) cubes. If bought in slices, the meat will be too thin to cube. Sliced meat may be cut into 5–8cm (2–3in) strips.

☛ Trim any excess fat from meat.

🍖 Use a saucepan with a heavy base for braising or stewing, thin-based saucepans will burn the bottom of the stew.

🍖 Choose a saucepan large enough to accommodate the amount of food to be cooked. For braising and stewing, the food should only half-fill the saucepan. For casseroling, the dish should be only two-thirds full.

🍖 When browning the meat cubes, heat only enough oil or butter to grease base of pan. Meat will not brown in a lot of oil, it will stew.

🍖 Brown over high heat, turn cubes with tongs, do not pierce with a fork. Brown a few pieces at a time only, to prevent the temperature of the pan dropping and juices running from the meat.

🍖 If browning in one pan and then transferring to a casserole or saucepan, remember to deglaze the pan – lift off the juices from the frying pan with a little stock, water or wine and add to the casserole.

🍖 Remember that long, slow cooking will tenderize the meat and develop a rich flavor, so plan to have the time available. Cooking the casserole or stew quickly will only toughen the meat. If time does not permit, finish cooking the next day.

🍖 If meat is to be coated with flour before browning, coat it, shake off excess and place straight into pan and brown. Avoid coating all the meat and piling it on a plate. Moisture from the meat will moisten the flour and make browning difficult.

☛ To store extra portions made in advance, use ziplock bags and store in freezer.

VEAL
PAN-FRYING VEAL

Suitable cuts: forequarter chops and steaks, loin chops and cutlets, leg steaks, rump steaks, eye of loin, schnitzel (cut from the topside of the leg)

POINTS FOR SUCCESS

☛ Season veal with pepper and herbs before frying. Add salt after cooking. As veal is mild in flavor, extra flavor can be added by:

☛ Cutting a large clove of garlic in half and rubbing cut surface over veal to give a faint garlic taste.

☛ Sprinkling veal with lemon juice and pepper five minutes before pan frying.

☛ Placing veal in a marinade before frying.

☛ Use a wide heavy-based pan that will accommodate the veal in one layer. If many pieces are to be cooked, keep the first batch hot by placing on a plate over a pan of simmering water, cover with a lid, overturned plate or foil.

☛ Serve pan-fried veal as soon as it is cooked.

☛ Thin veal steaks need only 1–2 minutes cooking on each side, depending on thickness. Overcooking will toughen the veal.

GRILLING VEAL

Suitable cuts: fillet, rump and shoulder steaks, forequarter chops, leg chops, loin chops, cutlets, eye of loin.

POINTS FOR SUCCESS

☛ Marinate the veal in an oil-based marinade, the oil prevents the veal from drying out. Extra flavor is also added to the meat. Brush with marinade during cooking.

☛ Best results are obtained with thicker cuts of veal.

☛ If thin veal steaks are to be grilled, marinate then cook for 1½–2 minutes on each side.

☛ If no marinade is being used, brush veal with oil before and during cooking to keep it moist and tender.

☛ For extra flavor, brush veal with onion or garlic juice before grilling. Add salt and pepper when placing under grill.

PAN-FRYING PORK

Suitable cuts: butterfly steaks, loin chops, pork medallions, forequarter chops.

☞ Use a heavy-based frying pan with just enough butter or oil to film the surface.

☞ Heat on a medium-high heat and add pork. Cook for 30 seconds to 1 minute on each side then lower heat to moderate and cook about 4 minutes on each side or until meat is springy to touch.

☞ If pork is crumbed, add oil or oil and butter to the pan to a depth of 3mm (⅛in). Heat well, add pork and brown both sides on brisk heat, then lower the heat and cook a further 3–4 minutes on each side to cook through. The pan may be partially covered with a lid to keep the pork moist.

☞ Remove pork and add a liquid to cover base of pan. Stir residue to lift pan juices and make into a light gravy to serve with pork.

STIR-FRYING PORK

Suitable cuts: diced pork, leg, shoulder, foreloin roast cut into dice, loin, fillet or schnitzel cut into strips or thin squares.

☞ Partly freeze meat before cutting into strips to make it easier to slice. Slice across the grain in very thin slices.

☞ Marinate pork before stir-frying to add moisture and flavor.

GRILLING PORK

Suitable cuts: medallions, butterfly steaks, loin chops, cutlets, leg steaks, forequarter chops, spare ribs.

☞ Remove rind from pork if not already removed. If you wish to cook it, cook separately under hot griller.

☞ Always cook pork under a medium heat. High heat will dry it out and make the pork tough.

☞ Grill pork approximately 5 minutes each side, according to thickness. To retain moisture, brush pork with a marinade or a little oil before and during cooking.

☞ Grilled pork must be served immediately.

BARBECUING PORK

Suitable cuts: forequarter chops, foreloin steaks, leg steaks, loin chops, spare ribs.

☞ Choose a thick chop or steak, thin cuts tend to dry out. Leg steaks and forequarter chops are ideal.

☞ Marinate pork for at least 30 minutes to keep pork moist and add flavor.

☞ Trim off excess fat and the rind. Fat drips into the coals and creates flames and smoke. Cook over medium heat, not hot, as pork will dry out and toughen.

☞ For kebabs and skewered pork, it is advisable to place on a wire rack which stands 1cm (⅓in) off the plate. The direct heat is too fierce for the small cubes.

LAMB

PAN-FRYING LAMB

Suitable cuts: loin chops, cutlets, chump chop, forequarter chops. Suitable cuts of trim lamb: butterfly, round and topside steaks or schnitzels, eye of loin, fillet.

POINTS FOR SUCCESS

☞ As forequarter and neck chops tend to be fatty, after cooking skim all the fat from the pan before using the pan juices to make the gravy. Otherwise the gravy will be very fatty.

☞ Cook thick chops on high for 1 minute on the first side, turn and cook for 1 minute, then reduce heat to medium or low for remaining time.

ROASTING LAMB

Suitable cuts: leg and shoulder, rack and crown roast, boned loin of lamb. Cuts of trim lamb suitable: eye of loin, neck fillet roast, round, topside, tunnel-boned leg, silvertop.

POINTS FOR SUCCESS

☞ It is important to skim any fat from baking dish before deglazing the dish and making gravy, otherwise the gravy may be very fatty. This is not necessary for trim.

LAMB ROASTS.

☞ Always place the roast fat-side down in the baking dish so that when it is turned half-way through cooking to fat-side up, it will brown and crisp.

BARBECUING LAMB

Suitable cuts: forequarter, leg, loin and chump chops, boned-out shoulder. Suitable cuts of trim lamb: butterfly, round and topside steaks, eye of loin, fillet.

POINTS FOR SUCCESS

☞ Cooking time for chops and steaks will vary with the thickness of the cut and the heat of the barbecue. About 4 minutes each side is a good guide. Sear meat on the hottest part of the grill then move to a more moderate part of the barbecue. If the fire is too hot, elevate the meat.

STARTERS

BEEF CARPACCIO

SERVES 4

500g (1.1lb) beef fillet
3 tablespoons extra-virgin olive oil
salt and freshly ground black pepper
125g (4oz) rocket leaves
1 tablespoon balsamic vinegar
Pecorino cheese shavings

☞ With a sharp knife, slice the beef into 5mm (⅕in) thick slices.

☞ Lightly oil a sheet of baking paper and season it lightly with salt and freshly ground black pepper.

☞ Arrange 4 slices of beef on this, approximately 5cm (2in) apart. Place another oiled piece of baking paper on top, and gently pound the meat until it has spread out to at least twice its former size. Repeat with remaining meat slices. Refrigerate until needed.

☞ Place rocket in the center of a plate, arrange the beef slices around the rocket. Drizzle with balsamic vinegar and remaining olive oil. Serve, topped with shavings of pecorino cheese and more black pepper.

BEEF TARTARE

SERVES 4

500g (1.1lb) fillet Mignon trimmed and diced
2 tablespoons extra virgin olive oil
2 tablespoons Dijon mustard
1 teaspoon Worcestershire sauce
2 tablespoons drained capers finely chopped
4 cornichons finely chopped
1 eschalot finely diced
Tabasco sauce to taste
salt and pepper to taste
4 egg yolks fresh as you can get
rocket leaves to serve
1 clove garlic cut in half
thinly slice baguette

☙ Place fillet in freezer till partially frozen, remove then cut into 5mm (⅛in) dice .

☙ In a mixing bowl combine oil, mustard, Worcestershire sauce, Tabasco and the diced fillet steak. Then add the cornichons, capers, eschalot, salt and pepper, combine well and refrigerate until needed.

☙ Arrange the rocket leaves on each plate and then use a cookie cutter lightly packed use a soup spoon to make an indent for the egg yolk then remove the mould.

☙ Toast the baguette slices and rub while warm with the halved garlic clove. Add the egg yolk to each dish just before serving.

LAMB BACKSTRAP WITH SWEET POTATO CHOPPED SALAD

SERVES 4-6

3 lamb backstraps
500g (1.1lb) rocket leaves and mixed leaves
2 sweet potatoes, cut into 1 cm (⅓in) cubes (to be roasted)
2–3 small beetroot, cooked and cubed
1 small red onion, finely sliced
75g (2.6oz) crumbled feta
3 bacon rashers, cooked and diced
50g (1.7oz) pine nuts, roasted
100g (3.50oz) roasted red capsicum (pepper), sliced into strips
barbecue rub of your choice
olive oil
salt and pepper, to taste
honey lemon mustard dressing
spiced avocado yogurt dressing

👁 Rub the lamb back straps with oil and barbecue rub let marinate for 30 minutes then on a hot grill cook for 3–4 minutes each side then rest for 10 minutes.

👁 If making your own dressings, prepare both the dressings and put them in the fridge until required. Or you can use store brand of your choice.

HONEY LEMON MUSTARD DRESSING

juice of ½ a lemon
2 tablespoons honey
3 tablespoons olive oil
2 tablespoons Dijon mustard
Salt and pepper, to taste

👅 Add all of the ingredients to a small jar and shake to combine.

Note: Store for up to 7 days in an airtight container in the fridge.

SPICED AVOCADO YOGURT DRESSING

juice of ½ a lemon
½ avocado
2 tablespoons chopped flat-leaf parsley
½ teaspoon coriander powder
salt and pepper, to taste
125g Greek-style yogurt

👅 In a blender, add all ingredients except for the yogurt. Blend until smooth, then add the yogurt. Stir to combine. Refrigerate until needed.

👁 Peel and cube the sweet potato, place in a large bowl then microwave for 4–5 minutes until tender, dress with enough oil to coat the potato and season with salt and pepper.

👁 Then place in a shallow oven tray on a medium hot barbecue with the hood down for 10–15 minutes or until browned, once done, set aside.

👁 On a medium hot barbecue cook off the bacon to your liking and set aside to dress the salad later. Slice the lamb back strap into thin slices then on a serving platter add the leaves, onion and toss, then top with the lamb slices, sweet potato cubes, beetroot, feta, capsicum and bacon.

👁 When ready to serve top with both the honey lemon mustard and spiced avocado yogurt dressing and pine nuts.

THAI BEEF SALAD

SERVES 4

6 lettuce leaves
500g (1lb) beef rump or tenderloin, roasted and sliced into strips
2 cloves garlic, finely chopped
1 Spanish onion, sliced
1 stalk lemongrass
¼ cup coriander (cilantro) leaves, torn
fried onion, to garnish
1 tablespoon dried chilli flakes, to garnish
1 cup of cherry tomatoes

DRESSING

4 kaffir lime leaves, cut into strips
3 cloves garlic, finely chopped
5 green chillies, seeded and finely chopped
1 tablespoon fish sauce
juice of 1 lime
50g (1⅔oz) palm sugar or brown sugar

👅 To make the salad dressing, combine all ingredients in a bowl (or jar) and mix well. To serve, arrange lettuce leaves on a serving dish, covering the whole surface area. Place strips of beef over lettuce, tomatoes and sprinkle over garlic, onion, lemongrass and coriander (cilantro).

👅 Add mint for more taste if desired. Pour the dressing over the top and garnish with fried onion and chilli flakes.

HALLOUMI WRAPPED IN BACON

SERVES 4-6

250g (½lb) Halloumi cheese
12 slices thin bacon
1 tablespoon barbecue sauce
basil for garnish

- Cut the cheese into 1cm (⅓in) square sticks.

- Wrap each cheese stick tightly in a slice of bacon.

- Cook in a fry pan on medium for 2-3 minutes/side or until bacon is crisp on all sides then using a brush coat in Barbecue sauce.

- Transfer to a plate, sprinkle with black pepper and garnish with basil.

BARBECUE MEATBALL SKEWERS

SERVES 4

oil, for cooking
1 onion, finely diced
500g (1lb) beef mince
1 egg
2 bacon rashers, finely diced
1 tablespoon barbecue sauce
1 tablespoon Worcestershire sauce
1 garlic clove, crushed
50g (1¾oz) panko breadcrumbs
salt and black pepper, to season

☛ If using bamboo skewers, soak in water for 20 minutes.

☛ Heat some oil in a frying pan over medium heat. Add the bacon and the onion then cook until the onion is soft and golden.

☛ Combine the remaining ingredients, ensuring that it is well combined, then roll into golf size balls.

☛ Place four balls on each skewer. Place the skewers on a medium–high Barbecue flatplate and cook for 8–12 minutes or until golden brown, turning every few minutes to brown all sides.

IN THE OVEN

ROASTED LEG OF LAMB

1 leg of lamb
2 cloves garlic, cut into slivers
2 fresh rosemary sprigs, cut into small pieces
salt and black pepper

👁 Add vegetables of your choice and cover lightly with oil

👁 Preheat the oven to 180°C (350°F). Make several incisions in the lamb using a sharp knife. Push the garlic slivers and pieces of rosemary into the incisions, then season well.

👁 Roast for 2–2½ hours until the lamb is tender, basting the lamb and turning the vegetables in the cooking juices every 30 minutes. Add a little more wine or water if necessary.

👁 Transfer the lamb to a plate, reserving the cooking juices, then cover with foil and rest for 15 minutes. Carve the lamb and serve with the vegetables, with the cooking juices drizzled over.

ROAST PORK

SERVES 4- 6

1 x 3kg (6½ lb) loin leg of pork
salt, to taste
apple sauce, to serve

👁 Preheat oven to 245°C (480°F). Rub pork with salt and place in a roasting pan. Cook pork in oven for 30 minutes to crisp crackling, then reduce heat to moderately slow (165°C/330°F) and cook for 3 hours.

👁 Continue to baste throughout cooking time. When pork is cooked, place in a carving tray and keep warm.

👁 Make gravy from pan juices.

👁 Serve roast pork with apple sauce, roast potatoes and roast vegetables.

ROAST BEEF

SERVES 6

1 x 1.5kg (3lb) rolled sirloin of beef
salt and freshly ground black pepper, to taste
butter or olive oil, for roasting

👅 Preheat oven to 165°C (330°F). Rub meat with salt and pepper and place in a roasting pan, fat side up. If the joint has little fat, add 1–2 tablespoons butter or oil to the pan. Place beef in the oven and cook for 2 hours.

👅 Remove roast beef to a hot carving platter and leave to stand in a warm place for 15–30 minutes before carving. This makes it easier to carve the meat.

👅 Serve with your choice of sides, vegetables or salad.

PORK BELLY IN THE OVEN

SERVES 4 -6

1kg (2lb) pork belly
1 tablespoon salt
1 tablespoon oil
Pepper to taste

☛ Preheat oven 240°C /460°F

☛ Score the rind with a knife, place the pork on a wire rack over the sink and pour a jug of boiling water over a towel, dry with a paper towel.

☛ Rub the skin with oil, salt and pepper.

☛ Place the pork on the rack into a baking tray in the oven and cook at 240°C (460°F) for 35 minutes or until skin crackles then reduce heat to 180°C (350°F) and cook for a further 25 - 30 mins.

☛ When done remove and rest for 10 minutes before cutting and serving.

MEATLOAF

SERVES 4 - 6

750g (1½lb) minced beef
45g (1½oz) breadcrumbs
1 onion, grated
75g (2½oz) carrot, grated
2 tablespoons capsicum (bell pepper) (optional), seeds and pith removed and finely chopped
60ml (2fl oz) tomato purée
60ml (2fl oz) milk
1 egg, beaten
2 tablespoons parsley, chopped
½ teaspoon mixed herbs
1½ teaspoons salt
freshly ground black pepper, to taste
chopped parsley, to garnish

☞ Preheat oven to 180°C (350°F). Place minced beef in a large bowl.

☞ In another bowl, blend together the breadcrumbs, onion, carrot, capsicum (if used), tomato purée and milk. Stir in egg, herbs, salt and pepper. Combine this mixture with the minced beef. Spoon meat mixture into a greased standard-sized loaf tin and bake in the oven for 1 hour.

☞ Drain off liquid, unmould onto a warm serving platter and serve garnished with parsley and accompanied by steamed vegetables and potatoes.

RACK OF LAMB

SERVES 2 -3

1 rib rack of 6 lamb cutlets, trimmed of fat
pinch of salt
mint jelly or mint sauce if desired

👁 Preheat oven to 165°C (325°F). Rub lamb with salt.
Place lamb on a rack in a roasting pan and cook in the
oven for about 45 minutes.

👁 Carve (on a board) into 6 cutlets and serve with mint
jelly or mint sauce or your vegetables of choice.

BEEF BOURGUIGNON

SERVES 6

2 tablespoons flour
1kg (2lb) stewing beef, chuck, blade or shin, diced
90g (3oz) butter
1 tablespoon tomato paste
2 garlic cloves, crushed
750ml (1½ pints) burgundy
625ml (20fl oz) beef stock
salt and pepper, to taste
1 bouquet garni
60g (2oz) pickled pork or bacon, diced
12 small onions
2 carrots, sliced
12 button mushrooms
chopped parsley, to garnish

Preheat oven to 165°C (330°F).

 Brown flour in a saucepan on medium heat for a few minutes until golden brown. Sprinkle diced beef with flour, then fry in a large pot with the butter for 5 minutes.

 Add tomato paste and garlic and cook for a further 5 minutes.

 Add burgundy and stock, season lightly with salt and pepper and add bouquet garni.

 Cover and cook in the oven for 2½–3 hours, or until tender.

 In a frying pan, fry pickled pork or bacon lightly. Add onions and carrots and cook over a moderate heat until evenly browned.

 Add pork or bacon and the mushrooms to the pot about 15 minutes before cooking is finished. Adjust consistency and seasoning if necessary and serve hot, sprinkled with chopped parsley.

Note: The traditional recipe has 2 tablespoons of brandy added in the final stage along with the mushrooms.

IRISH STEW

SERVES 4

1kg (2lb) potatoes, peeled
salt and pepper, to taste
1kg (2lb) lamb neck chops, trimmed of fat
500g (1lb) white onions, thickly sliced
bunch of herbs (parsley, thyme, rosemary)
1 carrot chopped
1 bay leaf
625ml (1¼ pints) beef stock
1 tablespoon extra parsley, finely chopped, to garnish

👁 Preheat oven to 165°C (330°F). Cut 3–4 potatoes into thick slices and cut remaining potatoes in halves.

👁 Place sliced potatoes in an ovenproof casserole dish and season with salt and pepper. Cover with meat, then add onions and halved potatoes, chopped carrot and season again. Add herbs, bay leaf and stock. Cover casserole dish and cook in the oven for 2–2½ hours or until meat is tender.

👁 Remove herbs and bay leaf from casserole and sprinkle with chopped parsley before serving.

STEAK PIE WITH GUINNESS

SERVES 4

3 tablespoons plain (all-purpose) flour
1 teaspoon English mustard powder
salt and ground black pepper
750g (1lb 10oz) stewing beef, trimmed & cut into cubes
4 tablespoons vegetable oil
2 onions, sliced
2 cloves garlic, finely chopped
2 cups Guinness
2 tablespoons Worcestershire sauce
2 bay leaves
4 sprigs fresh thyme, leaves removed & stalks discarded
1 teaspoon soft dark brown sugar
250g (9oz) chestnut mushrooms, halved if large

PASTRY

To make the Pastry

250g (9oz) self-raising flour
1 teaspoon salt
2 sprigs fresh thyme
freshly ground black pepper
125g (4oz) shredded suet

👁 Preheat the oven to 180°C (350°F). Combine the flour, mustard and pepper, then coat the beef in the mixture. Heat 2 tablespoons of oil in a heavybased frying pan. Fry a third of the beef for 3–4 minutes until browned. Transfer to an ovenproof dish, then fry the rest of the beef in 2 more batches and add to the dish.

👁 Add another tablespoon of oil to the pan, then fry the onions for 5 minutes. Add the garlic and cook for 2 minutes. Stir in the Guinness, Worcestershire sauce, bay leaves, thyme and sugar and simmer for 2–3 minutes.

👁 Pour over the beef, then cover and cook in the oven for 2 hours. Remove from the oven and increase the temperature to 190°C (375°F). Fry the mushrooms in the rest of the oil.

👁 Stir into the beef, then transfer to a 15 x 20cm (6 x 8in) pie dish.

👁 To make the pastry, sift together the flour and salt, then add the thyme and pepper. Stir in the suet and bind with 10–12 tablespoons of water to form a soft dough. Roll it out, dampen the edges of the dish and cover with the pastry. Trim, then make a small slit in the center. Cook for 30–40 minutes until golden.

SHEPHERD'S PIE

SERVES 4-6

500g (17½oz) minced (ground) lamb or beef mince
750g (1lb 10oz) potatoes, peeled and cut into chunks
1 teaspoon salt
2 tablespoons vegetable oil
1 medium onion, peeled and chopped
1 stick celery, diced
1 medium carrot, peeled and diced
1 tablespoon tomato purée
2 tablespoons Worcestershire sauce
¾ cup lamb stock
salt and black pepper
25g (¾oz) butter
¼ cup full-cream milk

☞ Remove lamb from refrigerator and bring to room temperature. Put the potatoes into a saucepan, cover with cold water and add the salt. Boil for 20 minutes or until tender.

☞ Meanwhile, preheat the oven to 200°C (400°F).

☞ Heat the oil in a large heavy-based frying pan over a medium heat, then fry the onion, celery and carrot for 2–3 minutes, until softened.

☞ Add the minced lamb to the pan, breaking it up with a wooden spoon. Cook for 5 minutes or until browned, stirring all the time. Stir in the tomato purée and Worcestershire sauce, mixing well.

☞ Cook for 2 minutes. Add the stock, stir, season to taste with salt and black pepper, then simmer for 5 minutes.

☞ Meanwhile, drain the potatoes and return them to the pan. Add the butter and milk, then mash until smooth.

☞ Spoon the mince mixture into a deep ovenproof dish, about 15 x 25cm (6 x 10in) in size. Top with the mashed potatoes, spreading them evenly and fluffing up the surface with a fork.

☞ Cook for 20 minutes or until the top is golden brown.

RED ROASTED PORK

SERVES 4

500g (1.1 lb) pork fillet
1 tablespoon sugar
1 tablespoon light soy sauce
1½ teaspoons black bean sauce
2 teaspoons salt
2½ tablespoons dry sherry
2 cloves garlic, crushed
1 teaspoon five spice powder
1 teaspoon red food coloring
1 tablespoon honey
1 tablespoon sesame oil

🍽 Cut pork into long strips, 4cm (1.58 in) thick. In a bowl, combine sugar, soy sauce, black bean sauce, salt, sherry, garlic, five spice powder and food coloring.

🍽 Add pork strips to marinate for at least 3 hours but preferably overnight, turning occasionally.

🍽 Preheat oven to 200°C/400°F. Transfer pork from marinade into a roasting pan and roast in oven for 15 minutes in a little oil.

🍽 Mix sesame oil with honey and spoon it over pork to roast for a further 15 minutes. After pork is cool, cut into thin slivers. Serve hot or cold.

THE FRY PAN

BEEF STROGANOFF

SERVES 4

90g (3oz) butter
1 large onion, thinly sliced
250g (8oz) mushrooms, peeled and sliced
750g (1½lb) fillet steak, trimmed of fat and cut into thin
strips
1½ teaspoons salt
freshly ground black pepper, to taste
pinch of nutmeg
300g (10oz) sour cream
parsley, chopped, to garnish

👁 Melt 60g (2oz) butter in a heavy frying pan and sauté
the onion until soft. Add mushrooms and cook for 5
minutes.

👁 Place mixture in a bowl and keep warm.

👁 Melt remaining butter in pan and quickly brown beef
strips on all sides. Do this stage in two lots unless you
have a very large frying pan. Take pan off the heat and add
onion, mushrooms, salt, pepper and nutmeg. Stir well to
blend, then replace pan over a medium heat and pour in
sour cream. Stir gently until heated through.

👁 Do not allow sauce to boil. Serve with plain rice.

BRAISED LAMB SHANKS

SERVES 2- 4

2 tablespoons olive oil
4 lamb shanks
1 onion, chopped
1 clove garlic (optional), crushed
1 carrot, diced
120g (4oz) celery, diced
200g (7oz) skinned, chopped tomatoes or tinned tomatoes
1 teaspoon salt
¼ teaspoon freshly ground black pepper
½ teaspoon sugar
60ml (2fl oz) beef stock or water
1 teaspoon Worcestershire sauce

👅 Heat oil in a frying pan and brown lamb shanks over a moderately high heat. Pour off most of the oil and reduce heat. Add onion, garlic (if used), carrot and celery and cook until onion is soft.

👅 Stir in tomatoes, salt, pepper, sugar, stock and Worcestershire sauce. Spoon some of the vegetable mixture over the shanks.

👅 Place a lid on the pan and simmer for 2 hours, or until tender.

👅 Serve with mashed potatoes and steamed vegetables.

CHILLI CON CARNE

SERVES 4

2 tablespoons olive oil
1 large onion, chopped
1 green capsicum (bell pepper), seeds and pith removed
and chopped
1 stick celery, chopped
1 tablespoon chilli powder (optional)
½ teaspoon salt
pinch of cayenne pepper
2 teaspoons paprika
500g (1lb) minced or diced beef
250g (8oz) tomatoes or 625ml (21fl oz) tomato pulp
250g (8oz) cooked kidney beans or soaked and cooked
haricot beans
150ml (5fl oz) water
add cheese and shallots if desired

👁 Heat oil in a saucepan. Add onion, capsicum and
celery and fry until just tender, then add other ingredients.
Bring just to the boil, lower the heat and cook gently
for about 55 minutes (for minced meat) or 1¼ hours
(for diced meat). Stir halfway through cooking, and add
a little more water if necessary.

👁 Serve in individual bowls or a large bowl with cheese
and shallots if desired, on top.

VIENNA SCHNITZEL

SERVES 4

500g (1lb) thinly cut veal steak, cut from leg
1 clove garlic, crushed (optional)
1 tablespoon lemon juice
salt and freshly ground black pepper, to taste
plain (all-purpose) flour, for coating
1 egg, beaten with 1 tablespoon water
breadcrumbs, for coating
olive oil, for frying
hard-boiled egg, anchovy fillets, capers, lemon slices and
parsley, to garnish

☞ Flatten veal between two pieces of plastic cling wrap,
using the side of a meat mallet or rolling pin. Cut skin on
edges to prevent curling during cooking. Lay veal on a plate
and set aside.

☞ Mix garlic (optional) with lemon juice and brush onto veal.

☞ Season with salt and pepper and allow to stand for
30 minutes. Dip each slice of veal into flour, then egg, and
finally breadcrumbs, pressing them firmly on to coat veal
completely. Refrigerate for 1 hour.

☞ Heat oil in a frying pan and shallow fry veal steaks over
a moderate heat for about 2 minutes on either side, or until
golden brown. Lift veal onto absorbent paper to drain, then
place on a hot serving platter. Garnish each schnitzel with a
slice of hard-boiled egg and top with a rolled anchovy fillet,
a few capers, lemon slice and parsley.

LESLEY'S MAGIC RISSOLES

SERVES 4

1 egg
60ml (2fl oz) milk
750g (1½lb) fine mince meat or chicken mince
60g (2oz) breadcrumbs
1 tablespoon red wine
1 carrot, grated
1 zucchini, grated
1 onion, grated
1 teaspoon soy sauce
dash of Worcestershire sauce
60g (2oz) flour
1 tablespoon butter

👁 Beat egg and milk together in a large bowl. Add mince and all other ingredients except flour and butter and mix well.

👁 Spread flour onto a cutting board. Form meat mixture into balls and roll in flour. Then flatten (with a spatula or knife) into rissoles and place on greaseproof paper. Continue until all mixture has been used.

👁 Heat butter in a frying pan over a low heat. Place rissoles in the frying pan and cook for 5 minutes, or until the bottom is golden brown, then turn and continue to cook for 10 minutes or until golden brown on the other side and cooked through.

👁 Serve with vegetables and mashed potato

PORK WITH MARSALA

SERVES 4

500–750g (1–1½lb) pork fillets, trimmed of fat
flour, seasoned with salt and black pepper, for coating
3 tablespoons olive oil
salt and freshly ground black pepper, to taste
1 tablespoon water
2 tablespoons plain (all-purpose) flour
125ml (4fl oz) Marsala
30g (1oz) butter

👁 Slice pork lengthways, almost through, so they form a butterfly fillet. Lay fillets open between 2 sheets of plastic cling wrap, and flatten with a meat mallet. Cut meat into pieces about 10 x 5cm (4 x 2in). Pound again until very thin, taking care not to break the slices. Dust lightly with seasoned flour.

👁 Heat oil in a pan and brown meat for 2 minutes on each side over a high heat.

👁 Sprinkle lightly with salt and generously with pepper, then remove meat from the pan and arrange slices overlapping on a warm serving dish. Keep warm. Add water to pan, then add flour and stir in, scraping up the crusty meat and flour leftovers. Pour in Marsala and stir until sauce is thickened and smooth, then add butter. When butter is melted, pour hot sauce over meat and serve.

STEAK DIANE

SERVES 4

4 slices of fillet steak cut 2.5cm (1in) thick
30g (1oz) butter
2 cloves garlic, crushed
salt and freshly ground black pepper, to taste
1 tablespoon tomato sauce
1 teaspoon Worcestershire sauce
60ml (2fl oz) water
1 teaspoon cornflour, mixed with a little cold water

👅 Slit steaks horizontally through to the center and open out meat to create a butterfly fillet. Flatten steaks with the side of a meat mallet to 5mm (¼in) thickness.

👅 Melt half the butter in a heavy frying pan, add 1 crushed garlic clove and fry the steaks quickly, about 40 seconds on each side for rare steak and 1 minute each side for medium steak.

👅 Add remaining butter and garlic to the pan when cooking the rest of the steaks (most frying pans will probably hold only two steaks at a time). Season cooked steaks with salt and pepper and keep aside on a warm platter.

👅 Add sauces and water to a frying pan and stir into pan juices over a medium heat. Thicken with cornflour paste and bring to the boil. Pour sauce over steaks.

👅 Serve with new potatoes and a tossed green salad.

VEAL OSSO BUCCO

SERVES 4

4 large veal shanks (osso bucco)
¼ cup seasoned flour
¼ cup olive oil
1 onion, finely chopped
1 clove garlic, crushed
¾ cup tomato pasta sauce
½ cup beef stock
400g (14oz) canned diced tomatoes
2 carrots, sliced
2 stalks celery, sliced
finely grated zest of 1 lemon, plus strips to garnish
400g (14oz) canned cannellinibeans, drained
¼ cup fresh parsley, chopped

👁 Coat the veal shanks lightly in seasoned flour. Heat
2 tablespoons oil in a large saucepan over medium–high
heat. Brown the veal shanks, then remove and set aside.

👁 Heat the remaining oil, add the onion and garlic
and cook for 2–3 minutes or until soft. Add the tomato
pasta sauce, stock, tomatoes, carrots, celery and lemon
zest. Return the veal to the pan. Cover and simmer for
35–40 minutes or until tender. Add a little more stock
if needed. Stir in the beans and parsley and cook until
heated through. Garnish with extra lemon zest. Serve with
mashed potatoes or polenta.

VEAL SALTIMBOCCA

SERVES 4

4 veal escallops, about 125g (4oz) each
50g (1¾oz) butter
250g (9oz) mozzarella, sliced into 8 rounds
8 slices prosciutto
½ bunch sage
½ cup white wine
¼ cup chicken stock

👁 Using a meat mallet, pound the veal until thin.

👁 Heat the butter in a pan, add the veal and brown quickly on both sides. Remove from pan, top each with 2 slices mozzarella, 2 slices prosciutto and 2–3 sage leaves. Secure with toothpicks.

👁 Under a hot grill, cook veal for approximately 2 minutes until cheese has just started to melt. Reheat the butter in the pan, add 2 teaspoons chopped sage and cook for 1 minute. Add the white wine and stock and simmer until the sauce has reduced slightly.

👁 Pour the sauce over the veal, and serve immediately.

SIZZLING BEEF

500g (17½oz) rump steak
2 tablespoons soy sauce
2 tablespoons rice wine or sherry
1½ tablespoons cornflour (cornstarch)
1 teaspoon sugar
3 tablespoons peanut oil
150g (5oz) broccoli, cut into florets
1 large red capsicum (bell pepper), cut into thin strips
2 cloves garlic, crushed
3 tablespoons oyster sauce
200g (7oz) bean sprouts
salt and black pepper

☛ Trim steak of any excess fat and cut into thin strips. Put the steak, soy sauce, rice wine or sherry, cornflour and sugar into a non-metallic bowl and mix thoroughly.

☛ Heat 1 tablespoon of the oil in a wok or large heavy-based frying pan, add one-third of the beef mixture and stir-fry over a high heat for 2–3 minutes, until browned. Remove and cook the remaining beef in 2 more batches, adding a little more oil if necessary.

☛ Heat the remaining oil in the wok, then add the broccoli and 6 tablespoons of water. Stir-fry for 5 minutes, then add the capsicum and garlic and stir-fry for a further 2–3 minutes, until the broccoli is tender but still firm to the bite.

☛ Stir in the oyster sauce, return the beef to the wok and add the bean sprouts. Toss over a high heat for 2 minutes or until the beef is piping hot and the bean sprouts have softened slightly, then season.

Note: Before you start cooking this colorful stir-fry, make sure all your ingredients are cut into pieces of roughly the same shape and size so that they cook evenly.

JAPANESE BEEF WITH HORSERADISH

SERVES 4

4 rump steaks, about 6oz (175g) each
4 tablespoons teriyaki or soy sauce
4 tablespoons olive oil
6 tablespoons crème fraîche
4 teaspoons horseradish cream
2 teaspoons peanut oil
7 scallions (spring onions), finely sliced, plus 1 scallion
(spring onion), shredded
2 cloves garlic, chopped
¼ teaspoon chilli flakes

👁 Pour over the teriyaki or soy sauce and olive oil and
turn the steaks to coat in a bowl. Cover and marinate for
1–2 hours in the refrigerator. Mix the crème fraîche and
horseradish in a small bowl, then cover and refrigerate.

👁 Heat a ridged cast-iron grill pan over a medium-high heat.

👁 Heat the oil in a heavybased frying pan. Add 2 steaks,
reserving the marinade, then cook for 3 minutes on each
side or until cooked to your liking. Remove and keep warm.
Cook the remaining 2 steaks, then remove and keep warm.
Put the sliced scallions, garlic, chilli and reserved marinade
into a small saucepan and heat through. Spoon over the
steaks and top with a dollop of the horseradish cream and
shredded scallions.

VEAL SCALOPPINE MARSALA

SERVES 4

4 very thin veal steaks, cut in half
salt and freshly ground black pepper, to taste
2 eggs, beaten
3 tablespoons plain (allpurpose) flour
45g (1½ oz) butter
125ml (4fl oz/½ cup) dry marsala or sherry
125ml (4fl oz/½ cup) beef stock

🥩 Season the veal steaks with salt and pepper. Dip the steaks in egg, then coat lightly with flour and set aside.

🥩 Melt half the butter in a frying pan. Add the steaks and brown the meat, for about 5 minutes on each side, taking care not to burn it.

🥩 When it is well browned, add half the marsala and swirl the steaks in liquid so that the liquid thickens with the flour and butter. Remove the steaks to warm plates. Repeat with the remaining steak fillets.

🥩 Add the stock and remaining butter to the pan. Scrape the base and sides to include all leftover bits in the sauce. Pour sauce over meat and serve.

SPICED SPARE RIBS

SERVES 4

1kg (2.2lb) meaty pork spare ribs
1 teaspoon Szechuan peppercorns
2 tablespoons cooking salt
½ teaspoon five spice powder
1½ tablespoons cornflour
oil for deep-frying

MARINADE

2½ tablespoons light soy sauce
2 teaspoons caster sugar
2 tablespoons dry sherry
black pepper, freshly ground
to garnish - parsley or coriander leaves (cilantro)

👁 Ask the butcher to chop spare ribs into 5cm (2in) pieces or use a sharp cleaver. Reserve.

👁 In a wok or heavy deep pan, stir-fry peppercorns with salt for about 5 minutes, stirring until salt colors. Remove. Then with mortar and pestle pound down peppercorns with five spice powder added.

👁 Combine marinade ingredients and set aside. Rub half of the spice mix into spare ribs with your hands, add marinade and turn each rib to ensure each is fully coated.

👁 Marinate for at least 3 hours, preferably overnight.

👁 Drain marinade from ribs and coat each rib with cornflour. Add more oil to wok until half full. Deep-fry ribs in batches over medium heat for about 4 minutes, remove, then re-fry until crisp and deeply golden.

👁 Drain ribs. Place on warmed serving dish, sprinkle with remaining spice mix and serve garnished with parsley or coriander leaves (cilantro).

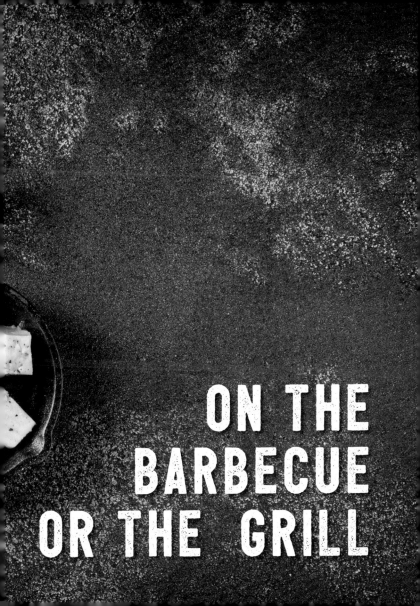

ON THE BARBECUE OR THE GRILL

SMOKEY BARBECUE SPARE RIBS

SERVES 4

2 x 1kg (2.2lb) racks American-style ribs
¾ cup smokey barbecue relish
¼ cup olive oil

☛ Place the ribs in a large, non-metallic dish. Thoroughly combine the relish and the oil and liberally brush onto the ribs.

☛ Cover and marinate in the refrigerator for several hours or overnight, turning occasionally.

☛ Take 2 large sheets of heavy-duty foil and place on a work surface. Place a rack of ribs on each. Generously cover both sides of ribs with extra marinade. Wrap into a double-folded parcel, making sure all joins are well sealed to prevent leakage. Carefully place the parcel onto a tray, taking care not to tear the foil. Refrigerate if not cooking immediately.

☛ Prepare the barbecue for direct-heat cooking. Place a wire cake rack on the grill bars to stand 25mm (1in) above the grill.

☛ Place the foil parcels on the rack and cook for 10 minutes on each side, a total of 20 minutes.

☛ Move the parcel to a plate. Open the foil and discard. Lift the ribs onto the rack. Continue cooking and brush with extra relish, turning until ribs are well browned and crisp, this should take about 10 minutes.

☛ Cut between the ribs to separate, pile onto a platter and serve immediately.

PORK ON A STICK

SERVES 4

1½kg (3.3lb) boneless shoulder of pork
1 cup teriyaki sauce
1½ cups Greek-style yogurt
8–10 bamboo skewers, soaked in water for 30 minutes
spring onions, sliced, to serve
½ cup chunky tomato relish

☞ Cut the pork into cubes. Place the cubes in a bowl and pour over the sauce to coat well, but keep a little to brush with while cooking. Cover and marinate in refrigerator for 1–2 hours or overnight to tenderize.

☞ Prepare the barbecue for direct-heat cooking and heat to hot. Turn a gas barbecue down to medium-hot when food is placed on. Place the pork skewers on the grill. Cook, turning and brushing with extra sauce for 12–15 minutes or until cooked to your liking.

☞ Serve skewers with spring onions scattered on top with chunky tomato relish in a dipping bowl.

BARBECUED BEEF RIBS

SERVES 4

1½kg (3.3lb) beef ribs
marinade
2 tablespoons soy sauce
6 tablespoons olive oil
2 tablespoons hot mustard
1 tablespoon lemon juice
½ teaspoon chilli powder
1 clove garlic, crushed
black pepper
1 onion, thickly sliced

👅 Cut ribs into serving pieces. Place in deep bowl.

👅 Combine soy sauce, oil, mustard, lemon juice, chilli powder, garlic and pepper.

👅 Pour marinade over ribs, and wedge a few slices of thick onions between pieces of beef.

👅 Marinate for 24 hours, turning from time to time.

👅 Barbecue over hot coals for about 20 minutes or until done. Serve with barbecue sauce.

STEAK WITH PEPPER SAUCE

SERVES 2

500g (1.1lb) rump steak, trimmed
freshly ground black pepper
salt, to taste

PEPPER SAUCE

½ cup fresh parsley, chopped
½ cup fresh chives, chopped
knob of butter
¼ cup cream

🍤 Prepare the barbecue and ensure it has a high heat.

🍤 Place the rump steak on the grill and lightly sprinkle with pepper. Cook until lightly browned, then turn and lightly sprinkle the other side with pepper.

🍤 To make the sauce, fry the parsley and chives with a knob of butter in a pan. Then add the cream. If you want a lot of sauce, add all the cream. If only a little sauce is required, add only half the quantity.

🍤 Serve the rump steak with sauce on the side, season with salt to taste.

T-BONE STEAK

SERVES 4

4 T-bone steaks
olive oil
salt and freshly ground black pepper
80g (3oz) butter, softened
3 cloves garlic, crushed
1 teaspoon Piri Piri seasoning
1 teaspoon parsley flakes

👅 Combine the butter, garlic, Piri Piri seasoning and parsley in a bowl. Mix together until smooth.

👅 Place the mixture onto cling wrap and roll into a tube shape. Place in the refrigerator or freezer until firm.

👅 Brush the steaks with olive oil and season with salt and pepper. Cook the steaks on the barbecue grill for 3 minutes each side or until cooked to your liking.

👅 Serve the steaks with crispy potatoes.

LAMB KEBABS

SERVES 4

750g (1.5lb) boneless lamb cut into 2cm (¾in) cubes
½ cup lemon juice
2 teaspoons fresh oregano
1 tablespoon fresh parsley, finely chopped
2 bay leaves, torn
1 small onion, chopped
¼ cup olive oil
ground black pepper
8 bamboo skewers, soaked

FOR SERVING

2 packets pocket pita breads
2 tubs tabouli
1 bottle chilli and garlic sauce

Place the lamb cubes in a bowl with the remaining ingredients. Mix to coat the lamb well. Cover and marinate in refrigerator for 2 hours or more. Thread 5–6 pieces of lamb onto each skewer. Retain the marinade. Take to barbecue area with breads, tabouli and remaining marinade.

Prepare the barbecue grill and heat to high and oil well. Place on the kebabs. Cook and turn when needed. Baste frequently with the remaining marinade. Cook for 4–6 minutes on each side. Meat should feel springy when pressed. Place the pocket pita breads at the side of the barbecue plate to warm up. Serve on a pita bread and spoon in a good serving of tabouli, add kebab skewer and a squeeze of the chilli and garlic sauce.

HONEY-GLAZED SPARE RIBS

SERVES 4

2kg (4.4lb) pork spare ribs, trimmed of excess fat
2 onions, chopped
2 tablespoons fresh parsley, chopped
1 cup chicken stock
2 tablespoons lemon juice
125g (4.4oz) butter, melted

SOY-HONEY MARINADE

4 small fresh red chillies, chopped
4 cloves garlic, chopped
2 spring onions, chopped
1 tablespoon fresh ginger, finely grated
1 ½ cup rice-wine vinegar
½ cup soy sauce
170g (5.9oz) honey

To make the marinade, combine the chillies, garlic, spring onions, ginger, vinegar, soy sauce and honey in a nonmetallic dish. Add ribs, toss to coat, cover and marinate in the refrigerator for at least 4 hours.

Drain the ribs and reserve the marinade. Cook the ribs, basting occasionally with reserved marinade, on a hot barbecue grill for 8–10 minutes or until the ribs are tender and golden.

Place on a serving platter, cover and keep warm.

Place the remaining marinade in a saucepan, add the onions, parsley, stock and lemon juice and bring to the boil.

Reduce the heat and simmer for 15 minutes or until sauce reduces by half. Pour the mixture into a food processor or blender and process to make a purée. With the motor running, pour in the hot melted butter and process to combine.

Serve the sauce with the spare ribs.

PORK STEAKS WITH MUSHROOM SAUCE

SERVES 4

4 pork shoulder steaks, trimmed of excess fat
freshly ground black pepper
1 tablespoon vegetable oil

MUSHROOM SAUCE

350g (12oz) closed cup mushrooms, sliced
1 clove garlic, crushed
1 teaspoon paprika
300ml (10.5oz) beef stock
1 tablespoon redcurrant jelly
1 tablespoon tomato purée
1 teaspoon cornflour
1 tablespoon water
2 tablespoons half-fat crème fraîche

🥩 Heat the barbecue to a high heat and oil the the grill. Season the pork steaks with pepper and sear for 1 minute on each side to brown, then cook for a further 5 minutes on each side or until tender and cooked through. Remove and keep warm.

🥩 To make the sauce, place the mushrooms and garlic in a fry pan and fry for 2 minutes or until softened. Stir in the paprika, beef stock, redcurrant jelly and tomato purée. Bring to the boil, then simmer for 5 minutes or until reduced slightly. Mix the cornflour with the water to form a paste, stir into the sauce and simmer for a further 2 minutes or until the sauce has thickened.

🥩 Take off the heat and then stir in the creme fraiche. And serve.

LAMB FILLET ROLL

SERVES 6-12

1 teaspoon ground cumin
1 teaspoon sweet paprika
½ teaspoon cayenne pepper
salt, to taste
1–2 lamb fillets
1 tablespoon olive oil
6-12 buns of your choice
3 small tomatoes, thinly sliced
1 cup baby spinach leaves
½ cup feta, crumbed

👁 In a shallow dish combine cumin, paprika, cayenne pepper and salt to taste. Coat the lamb fillet with the mixed spices.

👁 Prepare barbecue for direct-heat cooking. Heat until hot. Oil the grill bars, cook the lamb for 3–4 minutes each side for medium or to your liking. Remove from the heat and let the meat rest for 4 minutes before slicing the lamb diagonally into 1cm (⅓in) slices.

👁 Slice the buns in half lengthways. Add the tomato, spinach, lamb and some feta before serving.

MARINATED BARBECUE PORK CHOPS

SERVES 4

4 pork chops

MARINADE

3 tablespoons soy sauce
3 tablespoons Worcestershire sauce
3 tablespoons hoisin barbecue sauce
1 tablespoon balsamic vinegar
1 teaspoon garlic powder
1 teaspoon onion powder
salt and pepper, to taste

🥄 Trim the pork chops of rind and excess fat.

🥄 Place all the marinade ingredients into a large zip-lock bag. Add the pork chops and marinade for 1–2 hours or longer if possible.

🥄 Heat the barbecue grill, then cook the chops for 5–6 minutes on each side. For crosshatch grill marks, turn 45 degrees after 3 minutes.

🥄 Turn down the grill and baste with the leftover marinade until the chops are cooked through.

🥄 When done, cover with foil and rest for 5 minutes before serving.

LAMB KOFTAS

MAKES 10

9oz (25g) lean minced (ground) lamb
½ brown onion, finely diced
2 tablespoons couscous
2 sprigs mint, finely chopped
1 sprig parsley, finely chopped
2 teaspoons ground cumin
1 teaspoon ground coriander (cilantro)
1 tablespoon olive oil
pita bread and plain (natural) yogurt, to serve

👁 Soak wooden 10 skewers in water for 30 minutes.

👁 Combine all the ingredients in a mixing bowl. Mix together well, using your hands.

👁 Divide the lamb mixture into heaped tablespoonfuls. Use wet hands to shape each portion into a sausage. Thread each kofta onto a skewer and place on a baking (tray) sheet in a single layer. Cover and refrigerate for 1 hour or until firm.

👁 Cook the koftas on a preheated grill on the barbecue for 8–10 minutes, or until just cooked through. Turn and brush with olive oil occasionally. Serve with pita bread and yogurt.

KOREAN BARBECUE BEEF RIBS

SERVES 4-6

12 beef ribs, 7cm (just under 3in) long

MARINADE

360ml (12fl oz) soy sauce
45g (1½oz) sesame seeds, toasted
3 teaspoons sugar
1 teaspoon chilli
3 large cloves garlic, crushed

- Place the ribs in large plastic bag.

- Combine the soy sauce, sesame seeds, sugar, chilli and garlic and pour over the ribs.

- Press the air out of the bag and tie the top securely.

- Refrigerate for 4 hours, turning the bag over occasionally.

- Remove ribs and barbecue 10 cm (4 in) above the hot coals for about 15 minutes, or until the ribs are brown and crisp.

- Turn the ribs over occasionally.

FLANKEN CUT SHORT BARBECUE RIBS

SERVES 4-6

1.5kg (3lb) flanken cut short ribs
½ cup barbecue rub of your choice
1 tablespoon olive oil
½ cup barbecue sauce

🍖 Rub the ribs, ensuring they are well coated with the dry mixture.

🍖 Place the ribs in a single layer on a tray.

🍖 Cover and refrigerate for at least 2 hours (overnight is better).

🍖 Place the ribs on an oiled hot to medium barbecue grill.

🍖 Cook for 6 minutes on each side, then reduce the heat to low.

🍖 Brush with the barbecue sauce on each side until sticky and well coated with the sauce.

🍖 Rest for a few minutes before serving.

BARBECUE FLATTENED LAMB LEG

SERVES 4

1.5kg (2lb) lamb leg
2 garlic cloves, crushed
1 rosemary sprig, roughly chopped
2 tablespoons roughly chopped thyme leaves
3 tablespoons olive oil
½ tablespoon paprika
salt and black pepper, to season
3 lemons (1 to juice and 2 cut in half to garnish)

👅 Cut the lamb from the bone and cut to spread out flat (ask your butcher to do this to save time).

👅 Combine the lamb and all of the ingredients except the lemon halves in a large ziplock bag. Leave to marinate for at least 4 hours (overnight is better).

👅 Remove the lamb from the bag and using skewers, flatten out the lamb for cooking.

👅 Place the lamb on a medium barbecue grill, turning every 5 minutes, and cook for approximately 25–30 minutes for medium– rare or until cooked to your liking.

👅 Remove and cover with foil.

👅 Allow the lamb to rest for 10 minutes before slicing.

👅 Slice the lamb and place on a serving dish and grilled lemon halves. Squeeze the lemon onto the lamb at the table just before serving.

STEAK TACOS

SERVES 2-4

1kg (2¼lb) flank steak
3 tablespoons barbecue rub
2 tablespoons olive oil
1 tablespoon apple cider vinegar
6 x 15cm (6in) soft tacos
coriander, (cilantro) to garnish
1 lime, cut into wedges, to serve
1 jalapeño, finely sliced (optional)

🥩 Rub the flank steaks with the barbecue rub and place in a bowl or plastic bag with the olive oil and vinegar. Allow to marinate for at least 30 minutes at room temperature (overnight in the fridge will give better (results).

🥩 Cook the steaks on a medium–high barbecue grill for 3–4 minutes on each side for medium rare–medium, or to your liking.

🥩 Rest for 4 minutes, then slice into strips against the grain.

🥩 While the steak is resting, warm the soft taco on the grill (on low or turned off, depending on the heat of your grill).

🥩 Serve the tacos with the flank steak and salsa and some lime wedges on the side.

🥩 Garnish with coriander (cilantro). Add extra jalapeños if you are game.

PULLED PORK SANDWICH

SERVES 6-10

2 onions, sliced
3 bay leaves
4 teaspoons mustard powder
4 teaspoons smoked paprika
1½–2 kg (3–4lb) pork shoulder, boned with rind attached and tied (ask your butcher to do this)
150g (5oz) tomato sauce
90ml (3fl oz) red wine vinegar
20ml (½fl oz) Worcestershire sauce
12 teaspoons soft dark brown sugar
2 French sticks, sliced into rolls, and coleslaw to serve

Heat oven to 160°C (320°F).

👅 Add onions and bay leaves to a large roasting tin. Mix mustard powder, paprika and 1 teaspoon of ground black pepper with a good pinch of salt. Thoroughly rub this all over the pork.

👅 Place the pork, rind side up, on top of onions.

👅 Pour 210ml (7fl oz) water in to the bottom of the tin, wrap well with foil and bake for 4 hours.

👁 Light the barbecue. Mix tomato sauce, vinegar, Worcestershire sauce and brown sugar. Remove pork from tin and pat dry.

👁 Place the roasting tin on the hob, add tomato sauce mixture and bubble for 10–15 minutes until thick and glossy.

👁 Remove bay leaves and pour into a food processor; blitz until smooth. Smear half the sauce mixture onto the meat.

👁 Once the barbecue flames have died down, cook the pork, skin side down, for 15 minutes until nicely charred, then flip and cook for another 10 minutes.

👁 The meat will be very tender, so be careful not to lose any between the bars.

👁 Lift the pork onto a large plate or tray. Remove string and skin. Using 2 forks, shred the meat into chunky pieces.

👁 Add 60–90ml (2–3fl oz) of barbecue sauce and toss everything well to coat.

👁 Pile into rolls and serve with extra sauce and a little coleslaw.

INDEX

Barbecue Flattened Lamb Leg	118
Barbecue Meatball Skewers	37
Barbecuing beef	11
Barbecuing lamb	21
Barbecuing pork	19
Barbecued Beef Ribs	97
Beef	4
Beef Bourguignon	52
Beef Carpaccio	24
Beef Stroganoff	68
Beef Tartare	27
Braised Lamb Shanks	71
Braising, casseroling and stewing beef	13
Chilli Con Carne	72
Flanken Cut Short Barbecue Ribs	117
Grilling beef	11
Grilling pork	19
Grilling Veal	16
Halloumi wrapped in bacon	34
Honey-glazed Spare Ribs	104
In The Oven	39
Irish Stew	55
Japanese Beef with Horseradish	86
Korean Barbecue Beef Ribs	115
Lamb	20
Lamb backstrap with sweet potato chopped salad	28
Lamb Fillet Roll	108
Lamb Kebabs	103
Lamb koftas	112
Lamb roasts	21
Lesley's Magic Rissoles	76
Marinated Barbecue Pork Chops	111
Meatloaf	49
Mince beef	12
On The Barbecue Or The Grill	91

Oven-roasting beef 7
Pan-frying beef 4
Pan-frying lamb 20
Pan-frying pork 18
Pan-frying veal 15
Pork Belly in the Oven 47
Pork on a Stick 95
Pork Steaks with Mushroom Sauce 107
Pork with Marsala 78
Pulled Pork Sandwich 122
Rack of Lamb 50
Red Roasted Pork 64
Roast Beef 44
Roasted Leg of Lamb 40
Roasting lamb 21
Roast Pork 43
Shepherd's Pie 60
Sizzling Beef 84
Smokey Barbecue Spare Ribs 92
Spiced Spare Ribs 88
Starters 23
Steak Diane 79
Steak Pie with Guinness 56
Steak Tacos 121
Steak with Pepper Sauce 99
Stir-frying beef 6
Stir-frying pork 18
T-bone Steak 100
Thai Beef Salad 33
The Fry Pan 67
Veal 15
Veal Osso Bucco 80
Veal Saltimbocca 83
Veal Scaloppine Marsala 87
Vienna Schnitzel 75

First published in 2023 by New Holland Publishers, Sydney
Level 1, 178 Fox Valley Road, Wahroonga, 2076, NSW, Australia

newhollandpublishers.com

A record of this book is held at the National Library of Australia

ISBN : 9781760795931

Group Managing Director: Fiona Schultz
Designer: Ben Taylor (Taylor Design)
Production Director: Arlene Gippert

Printed in China

10 9 8 7 6 5 4 3 2 1

Keep up with New Holland Publishers

 NewHollandPublishers

 @newhollandpublishers